Praise for RIFQA

"Rooted in Palestine and ranging acros[s] ... [t]hat hurl themselves at the boundaries of wh... [t]hat put a premium on anger, that reflect the s... ...world today, that gift new and powerful phrases to the lexicon of liberation."
—AHDAF SOUEIF, author, *Cairo: My City, Our Revolution*

"*Rifqa* is an absolute marvel, and El-Kurd is precisely the kind of poet—Palestinian or otherwise—we need right now: unafraid of the truth. The legacy of his grandmother, the eponymous Rifqa, flits across these poems, and with it comes wisdom, hope, and, most crucially of all, memory. 'She left Haifa to go to Haifa / to go to Haifa,' he writes of his grandmother. This is a collection of remembering, not just the past but the unfolding present, one that is constantly facing erasure; of his own place in this lineage, he writes, 'What I write is an almost. / I write an attempt.' El-Kurd doesn't flinch from the violence and death that comes with dispossession. But make no mistake. These are the poems of the defiantly, unapologetically, wholly alive."
—HALA ALYAN, author, *The Arsonists' City*

"Witnessing Mohammed El-Kurd cut down dragons with the mere shift in his gaze has been a gift to our generation. Reading him is a journey into our collective pit of pain, of unreasonable loss, of screams unheard and unabating, of anger that he tells us '*even anger* is a luxury.' El Kurd's debut book of poetry is a self-portrait of a Palestinian child who has grown up besieged by nuclear-backed settlers in his own home, protected, still, by his beloved grandmama Rifqa's indomitable belief that her family and her people would prevail. *Rifqa* is an admixture of the most intimate violence—wounds that are as difficult to reveal as they are to heal—together with song and dance that beseech the sun to sustain this life and these lands that ensure it. Rifqa El-Kurd lives in Mohammed and Mohammed breathes life into us, scented with fire and jasmine flowers, so that we may know her, and the victory she embodied, too."
—NOURA EREKAT, author, *Justice for Some: Law and the Question of Palestine*

"*Rifqa* is the collision of strength and vulnerability. Earnest in its exploration of the grave realities in one corner of the globe, it is a banging on the doors of the world. It illustrates the wit that is necessary to weave together the tragic with the hopeful and the painful with the joyful. *Rifqa* is a testament to overcoming fear in expression, a book that will resonate with you, one you hold and return to over and over again."
—MARIAM BARGHOUTI, journalist, researcher, activist, and commentator

"Palestinians have long fought with poetry. Napoleon's army in Palestine was defeated by warrior poets. El-Kurd's words are part of this long and dazzling lineage. An elegy to our ancestors, maternal, whose resistance we hope to honor, each poem is a rock hurled at the occupier and the oppressor. A beautiful and important book."
—RANDA JARRAR, author, *Love Is an Ex-Country*

"At its heart, *Rifqa* is a call to build a better elsewhere for Palestinians, in & beyond language: an ars poetica beyonded into unity intifada, where Palestinians are loved into present tense. Beyond a failed imagination of poetry that's more 'theater over thunder,' beyond a poetics where elegy is merely a symptom of border, Mohammed El-Kurd weaves the ancestors and Land into every breath of these poems. 'Every grandmother is a Jerusalem,' El-Kurd reminds us, in jasmine-scented memory, in liminal space and punch line, in auto- and anti-biography. Here is poetry the whole of us can turn and return to—even in grief, even in contradiction. Liberating itself from respectability & other colonialist gazes weaponized against Palestinians, here is poetry insistent on truths we've carried for generations. JERUSALEM IS OURS. El-Kurd writes this with its whole chest, knowing our lives—the whole & future of us—depend on it."
—GEORGE ABRAHAM, author, *Birthright*

RIFQA

MOHAMMED EL-KURD

Foreword by aja monet

Haymarket Books
Chicago, Illinois

Published in 2021 by
Haymarket Books
P.O. Box 180165
Chicago, IL 60618
773-583-7884
www.haymarketbooks.org
info@haymarketbooks.org

ISBN: 978-1-64259-586-4

Distributed to the trade in the US through Consortium Book
Sales and Distribution (www.cbsd.com) and internationally
through Ingram Publisher Services International (www.ingram-
content.com).

This book was published with the generous support of Lannan
Foundation and Wallace Action Fund.

Special discounts are available for bulk purchases by organizations
and institutions. Please email info@haymarketbooks.org for more
information.

Cover artwork by Monther Jawabreh.

Printed in Canada by union labor.

Library of Congress Cataloging-in-Publication data is available.

10 9 8 7 6 5 4 3

For my grandmother, Rifqa El-Kurd,
and for occupied Sheikh Jarrah

Contents

Foreword
Love Is Older Than "Israel"

I first learned of Mohammed and his grandmother, Rifqa, through a documentary film we watched in East Jerusalem (East Jeru). We were a delegation of Black American movement organizers and artists. It was January 2015. The cold tapped bone. We huddled into a room to listen and learn, to feel and be connected, to organize. We visited Rifqa and Mohammed's home in Sheikh Jarrah, where colonizing settlers had once forcibly entered and pushed their family to the back. Our delegation bore witness and asked what more could be done. "Go back home and tell the world what you've seen here."

Rifqa wasn't asking a favor; it was a deafening command for American awareness and accountability. Our charge was to tell their story, to amplify their voices, and to be present with the people. No one could have prepared me for what I saw with my own eyes and felt with my own heart. You cannot unsee once you have seen. I thought I was a radical poet before, but Palestine uprooted any sense of who I thought I was. I became more me, more true, more fearless. I saw the audacity of evil and how it can be rationalized. Palestinians are not the only people to suffer at the hands of settler colonialism and Western white terrorism. Yet we cannot afford to stay quiet about what is taking place there. The state of Israel and the justification for its existence are a crimes against all of humanity. The state is the worst of the human spirit manifested into a fully functioning government.

Tell them, "America is the reason."
—from "The Biggest Punch Line of All Time," p 85

It is now 2021, and I have the honor of writing the forward to Mohammed El-Kurd's first book of poems, *Rifqa*. I do not need to tell his story for him. He has been telling his own story for many years, and now the world is finally starting to listen. The culture is shifting, and we are seeing the results of years of organizing for this shift to occur. Still, liberation is not a media strategy. It is a matter of life and death. As a child born on the day of the Nakba, what would Mohammed seek to be except a testament, a siren, a freedom song conjuring a key that fits a hole in a heart the size of Falasteen, from the river to the sea. Mohammed is a daring breath, a blessing that raises the dead. With soft-spoken political finesse, these poems choose voice. They embrace the urgent life of words in service to the emotional landscape of resistance. Unsettling the colonial project of lies, Mohammed is a truth teller. He wields his arsenal: a living room of poems seats us in the home of what remains, what cannot be photographed or tweeted but is in the spirit of enduring strength, the will to fight, to create, and, most importantly, to love.

> *What I write   is an almost*
> *I write   an attempt.*
> **—from "Rifqa," p 17**

There is what words can do, and there is what is beneath the words: the fire and fury of what willed them into existence. There is what we hope they will do, and there is what they have actually done. Mohammed writing from the front lines of occupied Palestine is an action, a doing, a done. I think about how I love him and how his words have held me. Advocating for this book is one small way I have chosen to demonstrate my solidarity. We are made up by those we love, and it is by our relationships with people that we are transformed. Solidarity is a feeling and a doing. It is a series of choices we make with one another. It can only be felt. It cannot be contrived or manipulated. Solidarity is not just about our shared pain or struggle but also, most importantly, about our shared joy, visions, and dreams. It is an energetic force and a resounding love.

Mohammed always wanted to publish a book of his poems. Here is a dream he shared with me, and now it is our dream together. He is a powerful poet and activist, and he is also my friend.

We will continue to struggle, but we are who we love and live by in spite of that struggle. Poetry sees us for who we truly are, and what is in that reflection must be faced. Poetry is a home for the dispossessed; it is our belonging. Rifqa is my grandmother, and she is your grandmother, too. We are the grandchildren of her fight, her fierce and enduring love—her poetry. May these poems challenge and awaken you. May they shake you into action. May they help you find the words for what you already know to be true. We cannot afford to be silent. Mohammed's poems confront and reveal us.

> *What do you say to the children for whom the Red Sea*
> *doesn't part?*
> **—from "No Moses in Siege," p 31**

Mohammed shows us how poets are made. A poem is a life, and a life is a poem that calls us inward. What a poem becomes in our innermost spaces is a land that cannot be owned, though it can be cared for, tended to, and loved. It is a relationship that shifts and changes with the seasons, a howl that knows us by name and need. May we see ourselves in these poems and steward their truths. The freest people on earth are not controlled by hatred or fear but moved by love and truth. We are more than what was done to us; we are who we've become in spite of it all. Who do we choose to be, and what will we do about it? Mohammed El-Kurd shows us a way.

I walk the world with his words tattooed on my right leg: "I cried not for the house but for the memories I could have had inside it." These words remind me that home is a series of shared memories, not brick and mortar. Home is where we go to remember and revisit who we've always been. Mohammed El-Kurd's poetry is a home returned to us. His poems call us home.

Always,
aja monet

As I write this, our family lawyer is attempting to persuade a settler judge to rule against settlements: a zebra at the mercy of a jury of hyenas.

I am Sheikh Jarrah.
There's a spear in my waist
and spears in my back.
My resilience is an edifice.
I am Jerusalem's northern gate.
When treachery occurs,
I am fields of coal
and the wind will certainly blow
in the direction my ships covet.
—Maysoon Abu Dweih El-Kurd

ONE

In Jerusalem

God has become a refugee, sir.
—Rashid Hussein

"Fireworks or bombs?"
Loren often asked
in fresh, concerned American breath.
I'd respond with "A wedding, probably,"
or "There are no weddings in December."

After she's worn Jerusalem
and been worn by it,
"Fireworks or bombs?"
Loren asks. A giggling tornado
escapes our mouths
touched by our numbness
in fatal ways.

My mother has always said:
"The most tragic of disasters
are those that cause laughter."

WHO LIVES IN SHEIKH JARRAH?[1]

As a boy, I lived in Sheikh Jarrah, a
Jerusalem. Annexed
by

everything
Israeli
over the last six decades,
slowdown   Israeli
construction in   Jerusalem,

going   at full speed.

a jewish
state now runs through
Jerusalem

I
halt
hope

my father,

lived in   Palestin   e   but ev-
ery day
the   checkpoint   divided

both sides.
Sheikh Jarrah was a

refugee

Sheikh Jarrah   my youth is
gone;
razed by Israeli
bulldozers

Jerusalem
remains   Is-
raelis venture   Sheikh Jarrah and the
neighborhoods
Jerusalem,   Palestinians

Today   Jerusalem
a city occupied by a foreign
power.   it is

Prime Minister

is   a
settlement
all Israelis

Colonialism in

Jerusalem killed the
peace

For
thousands,   Palestinians
have been   in Sheikh Jarrah
Friday   the expulsion
Israeli courts
violent demon
legal
police

cruel
the   Palestinians
in Sheikh Jarrah
were   originally   expelled   in
1948 from
the
wake   Israeli courts
ruled   these
refugees
are

stubborn

---

1 Erasure of an article with the same name, published in the *New York Times*,
April 2010.

Born on Nakba Day[2]

Your unkindness rewrote my autobiography
into punch lines in guts,
blades for tongues,
a mouth pregnant with
thunder.

Your unkindness told me to push
through,

look,
listen.

I was born on the fiftieth anniversary of the Nakba
to a mother who reaped olives
and figs
and other Quranic verses,
watteeni wazzaytoon.[3]
My name: a bomb in a white room,
a walking suspicion
in an airport,
choiceless politics.

I was born on the fiftieth anniversary of the Nakba.
Outside the hospital room:

---

2 The term Nakba (Arabic for catastrophe) refers to the occupation of 78 per-
cent of Palestine through ethnic cleansing and massacres and the creation
of "Israel" on that territory in 1948. The Palestinian people commemorate
the Nakba on May 15th every year. Though defined by historians as the war
that took place between 1947 and 1949, many argue that the Nakba is still
ongoing, as the Zionist settler-colonial project continues to kill, dispossess, and
displace Palestinians. (For more information, see Grassroots al-Quds.)

3 Quran, 95:1: "By figs and olives."

protests, burnt rubber,
Kuffiyah'ed faces, and bare bodies,
stones thrown onto tanks,
tanks imprinted with US flags,
lands
smelling of tear gas, skies tiled with
rubber-coated bullets,
a few bodies shot, dead—died
numbers in a headline.

I
and my sister
were born.

Birth lasts longer than death.
In Palestine death is sudden,
instant,
constant,
happens in between breaths.

I was born among poetry
on the fiftieth anniversary.
The liberation chants outside the hospital room
told my mother
to push.

This Is Why We Dance

for Carmel

Home in my memory is a green, worn-out couch
and my grandmother in every poem:
every jasmine picked off the backlash,
every backlash picked off the tear gas,
and tear gas healed with yogurt and onions,
with resilience,
with women chanting, drumming
on pots and pans
with *goddamn*s and *hasbiyallah*s.

They work tanks, we know stones.

2008, during the Gaza bombings
my ritual of watching TV
ran between grieving
and Egyptian belly dance music.
I fluctuated between hatred and adoration,
stacking and hoarding Darwish's reasons to live
              sometimes   believing them,
              sometimes dipping my bread in indulgence,
knowing a child is breadless, in Khan Yunis,
dipped in a roof's rubble . . .

If you ask me where I'm from it's not a one-word answer.
Be prepared   seated,   sober,   geared up.
If hearing about a world other than yours
makes you uncomfortable,
drink the sea,
cut off your ears,
blow another bubble to bubble your bubble and the pretense.
Blow up another town of bodies in the name of fear.

This is why we dance:
My father told me: "Anger is a luxury we cannot afford."
Be composed, calm, still—laugh when they ask you,
smile when they talk, answer them,
educate them.

This is why we dance:
If I speak, I'm dangerous.
You open your mouth,
raise your eyebrows.
You point your fingers.
This is why we dance:
We have wounded feet but the rhythm remains,
no matter the adjectives on my shoulders.

This is why we dance:
Because screaming isn't free.

Please tell me:
Why is anger—*even anger*—a luxury
to me?

Girls in the Refugee Camp

A soldier
  hands you hash
   and handcuffs.
Van
   coffins your spine.

Road
   takes you where it takes you.
Many prisons in the journey,
  seldom doves at the destination.

You are Damascus and
you are the gate.

Born on the brink of a breath.
  On the brink of a death,
pain teeths in your mother.
Your throat's a minaret.
The hospital bed—a prayer rug;
allahu akbar,
your family announces
   your boyhood
  and your doom.

Birth begins to halve you.
You are a cliché in the wind:
      lipstick on a mirror,
  shrouds
  in leopard print
  bricks thrown, rung.
       Your tongue genders
       as it needs
       in barbershops and bureaucracy—
thick voice from a vending machine
    softens at the ring of a phone.

Your father was a bullet away
      before a bullet took him,
came home a martyr
         never a father.
    You were destined,

   the man you are an orphan,
and you are the womb.

Body—a storm in waiting rooms
frowning, spitting,
       sitting in a whirlpool,
waiting on rhythm to resurge
     on surgeries to affirm
     on gavels to blow
in favor of your truth.

Sky here is made of tin,
                    children
drive taxis and drive their bread,
prostitute gum on traffic stops,
faces
              smug
windows
          rolled up.
Your ambition is ammunition
bullet-less.

You are the poor and
you are outside of the gate.

But your hands don't open.
    Your hunger does not announce.
    You move what you move to move up
   You doubt who you doubt.

Soldier
  hands you hash
       and handcuffs,
hijacks your halves.

You are the prisoner and
you are the cell.

Bulldozers Undoing God

for Mahfoutha Ishtayyeh

A chain is corseting
the tree's waist and hers,
flesh in flesh,
      olive skin on olive skin,
fingers   branches   intersections
    rootedness jars their storms,
             wraps them
in her unbreakable word
         we will not leave.
             Leave!

She clings onto the tree trunk
      the feeling afore the drown.

Land   stone and dirt, pillowed
      buried ones and ones lying
      contaminated reality
      numbed faith, indulged upon
      embroidered destinies
      constant Nakbas
      tragedy pillowed and bedroomed
made normal: mornings of mourning
on a breakfast table,
      olives
      za'atar
      tomatoes and cucumber
      tragedy
      tear gas and tea

In Jerusalem, every footstep is a grave.

This was only love:
her skeleton is that of the tree's,
roots stitched into land into identity.
Separation is like

        unmaking love
        ungluing names to places
        undoing God.

            A pulling pressure, soldiered:
            occupiers occupy her limbs,
            untangling a grandmother.
        A soldier as old as a leaf born yesterday
pulls a trigger on a woman older than his heritage.

            Two martyrs fall.

                One
                martyr
                falls.

        Here, every footstep is a grave,
every grandmother is a Jerusalem.

Smuggling Bethlehem

I am no stranger to picking apples out of men's throats.
Atlanta
I'm tired of making amends with soon-to-be strangers.
Tired of being my mother's favorite stranger.

I am her fingers rolling grape-leaves till they taste like a fire pit
warming my exile, muffling my diaspora.
Hookah out of honeyed apples, smoke where once was sex.

In my lonely I spend time
shoving ghosts off of balconies. I go to war in a book.

In America, I sit in a coffin's throat
thinking of birds picking
                    pink almond blossoms from bullet-wounded trees.

In Palestine,
                                        strangers
walk around with open purses
        open pockets
        open palms,
trusting the ruckus will affect everything but the integrity
of those wrinkled around them,
        selling olives, figs ,
                    and words wrapped with play.

Jerusalem strangled   with strangers,
virus   at the depths of its throat   cough
                    blood
                                        debris as if confetti.
They tell us to taunt tanks with resumés not rocks.

My mother knows how to place a fist in a man's arrogance,
   knows how to place silence in a bulldozer's mouth.

Mother picks apples from forbidden cities,
   hiding produce under her car seat,
   smuggling Bethlehem between her feet.

"وَجَعَلْنَا مِن بَيْنِ أَيْدِيهِمْ سَدًّا
وَمِنْ خَلْفِهِمْ سَدًّا
فَأَغْشَيْنَاهُمْ فَهُمْ لَا يُبْصِرُونَ"4

She breezed through the military barrier
what the soldiers call a checkpoint
a soldier deceived—
his throat
      picked
      harvested.

---

4 Quran, 36:9: "And We have put before them a barrier / and behind them a barrier / and blinded them, so they do not see."

A Song of Home

I inherited my father's stubbornness,
books I hid beneath my mattress,
bodies I wished to blanket
and notions I believed to be true
even when I lied and held on
even when I lied and was made to hold on
I believed to be true, possible,
the face of earth
before dawn, when my mother picked figs
prayed *allahu akbar*
and when she shelved her screams,
sipping tea with meramiya.
Mother and the sage were daughters of the mountain;
the quiet they offered, sometimes.
Somewhere along
reluctance to mirrors
a scream at the dinner table
a dish broken, accidentally or not
louder than bullets outside
even the TV screen filled with victims
didn't break the news of us
breaking
until somebody's body fainted
forcing them to hold down the arguments
barefoot,   I
was dragged into cars and dragged into points of view.
I talked to God but God never wore my shoes.
Sing me a song of home
break a dish or two   throw a stone or two
because the screams make me nostalgic:
I almost don't fear the sirens.

Portrait of My Nose

Arrogant with height.
One nose away from clouds.

I have my grandmother's
and in the knot, tangled
a homesickness
for people generous with
    nose.

My grandmother's is beautiful; mine is
one nose away from beauty,
one   away from Anglo-Saxon.

I have my grandmother's
and my grandmother had pride
favored functionality
she was never a
    nose away from anything
    but jasmines.

Rifqa

I see you standing like the cedars, standing
at the height of my memory, in the green of the moon.
I see you coming like the wind, coming.
The door falls beneath the wind and rain.
                    —Mahmoud Darwish

Nowadays, grandmother walks fragile,
so unlike the past she battled.

Wrinkled faces
hide inside the wrinkles of her face,
tell the story of that event:
  organized   undying.

The morning of a red-skied May   1948.
Could've been   today.
    They knocked the doors down,
claimed life as their own.
    The chances of their staying   fragile.
But now look:
      houses are in ruins,   keys around necks,
            odds far from even,   far from running water.

Ramadan   villages retired singing,
rifles sang instead,
announcing   declaring
an anticipated empire on the ruins of another.

Seven decades later
they harvest   organs of the martyred,
feed their warriors our own.[5]
The people of Haifa left.
Some fled after news   some stayed,
   gave coffee to massacre.
Some   walked a straight line into the sea
          back to their city
                    refused to be martyred
                    refused to exit.

They were one with Haifa,
drowned
      in this life,
      soaked in salt.

My grandmother—Rifqa—
was chased away from the city,
   leaving behind
          the vine of roses in the front yard.
Sometime   when youth was
          more than just yearning,
She left poetry.
What I write   is an almost.
   I write   an attempt.

She left behind   clothes   folded   ready to be worn again;
her suitcases
did not declare departure.

---

5 In 2009, Swedish photojournalist Donald Boström published an essay titled
"Our Sons Are Being Plundered for Their Organs," in which he exposed the
decades-long Israeli practice of returning the bodies of young Palestinian men
to their families with organs missing. See also: Israeli necroviolence.

Rifqa left Haifa   to go to Haifa
to go to Haifa.
Rifqa walked solid.
"We'll return once things cool down,"
and she believed,
wore her key
until her key   her neck   her memory
            became the same color.

Next stop   another city-to-be-destroyed,
photographs of Haifa stamped on her heart,
                then on my imagination.

She went   shelter to shelter.
    I wonder, was it the shelter that ran from her?

Children along the way,   six
storied them their homeland,
and so   they grew up
singing songs of arrival,
      the songs of homecoming.

1956

lucky refugees   given houses
lucky   wrapped in the shiny promises of
UNRWA   the Jordanian government grandma
a lucky refugee   grew vines of roses around the house;
      this time the roses had thorns
           just in case.

Invaders   came back once again,
      claimed the land
with   fists and fire   excuses beliefs
of the chosen and the promised
as if God is a real-estate agent.

Sometime she became   a thirty-something-year-old widow
homed half a dozen hungers
       denied hers
She worked,
   worked,
 and worked
until survival was a funny story to tell
on evenings   with
      what remains of the family.

1967   another Nakba
            another man-made catastrophe
                names of places   dispossessed
                names on tombstones   rewritten
Sheikh Jarrah became Shimon Ha'tsiddik
Jerusalem
        bride of the fantasy
                once more.

Years passed and the vines of the roses
        were   vines of grapes,
           vines of barbed wires,
ripping open the veins of this city.

Years passed   children
became my aunts   my father
the twenty-first century   didn't stop the Nakba
from continuing   years of resistance
popular   fever and rashes
unable to stop this cancer from spreading.

May 15, 1998,
I was born before a closed house
that I called mine but have never been in.
          After nine years of fines
paychecks and playchecks
it was opened   for them
                                        not us.
The colonizers   youthful   differently clothed
rifles smacking against their hips   terrorist nation
celebrated stolen property   callous.
I cried—not for the house
but for the memories I could have had inside it.

Maha   three-year-old sister   cried her innocence,
watched the Zionist settlers burn her bed,
yet another Nakba
      another divine crime scene.
now Maha's eight.   She knows her Nakba isn't the first,

she knows   she's not the only child whose bed was burned,
she knows   children are burned.
Mohammad Abu-Khudair,   sixteen   gasoline.

With every lid closed
Rifqa went to her house

                          saw nothing
in the gray of her eyes   said,
Let's say it was devoured by the sea.
Don't worry   *it will wash ashore.*
"No matter how deep it drowns,
the truth always washes ashore."

She prays to her refuged God.

Nowadays she walks fragile,
so unlike the past that she battled,
so unlike the past
nameless faces
               remembered

                              on her wrinkled face.
They tell the story   of the particular events:
           organized, plural,

ongoing.

TWO

Wednesday

A man wailing is not a dancing bear.

—Aimé Césaire

There's death in the eyes of this newborn.
I heard the baby complain about a treacherous defeat,
called it *the same old catastrophe.*
A storm in his ear says it's raging for silence.
Thunder erupts when he's shushed.
What a worsened scenario. He skipped ahead.
What do you do when your destiny is predetermined?

Life in this hospital laughs at us.
Long is the wait. Wild is the wind.[6]
I ask if there's a wedding going on.
The nurse complained of the clouds.
If I were a stupid flower, I'd wither under the rain.
They asked her, *What's wrong with the flower?*
not *What's wrong with the rain?*

---

6 After Nina Simone's record.

Do not reconcile
even if they gift you gold.
If I were to gouge out your eyes
and place gems in their place
would you still see?

—Amal Dunqul

On the same day fifty years later,
there was a Friday in my eyes.

Mother was grateful she said no
to doctors running with scissors.
What a coincidence
both sisters
promised defective births.
My aunts cried comedy before conspiracy.

Grandmother told me she'd been pregnant
on the same day, fifty years before,
considered herself lucky
having escaped the knife.

It is the same killing;
they do it in whispers. Fifty years later,
I worry about my little brother.
He is six-foot-fear.
Eighteen-year-old soldiers
with rifles rivaling their torsos
shoot to kill.

28   It's the same killing
everywhere.
Seventy-some years later
we haven't lived a day.

Fifteen-Year-Old Girl Killed
for Attempting to Kill a Soldier
(with a Nail File),
or Context

In its bare reality, decolonization reeks of
red-hot cannonballs and bloody knives.
—**Frantz Fanon**

Context: fruit knife to a firearm. He was in her throat.
Fifteen-year-old girl denounced. *Violence* is not
children taking on dragons.

For me, it has always been apologies.
Running to catastrophe with context,
commissioning compassion, turning
heroes into humans. This is a refuted revolution.

TV said her brother was a martyr,
but martyrs go with intent. He went
bullet to the head. From fist to flounder.
Context is hand in his pocket. Toy guns.

I told the people that day, disclaimer:
dead girl shouldn't have found her rage
in the kitchen drawer. She was reaching for crayons.
Solidarity often is a refuted revolution.

I held my arsenal.
People who give excuses for executions
fear the rifle more than they fear the reason.
I put her in tulle—girl to their gaze,
angel to their accusations. Otherwise

nail file becomes the villain, despite
context. Context: they want cats
declawed, they want knocked doors
unanswered, they want the other cheek.

Terrorist Avenges. Headlines delusional.
Are all heads equal?[7] Is a soldier's heart
equal to her brother's? I'll hold my arsenal.
When they ask me next time,
I'll say God held her hand.

---

7 After Amal Dunqul.

No Moses in Siege

*On July 16, 2014, four boys—aged between nine and fourteen—
were killed by Israeli naval fire while playing soccer on a beach in
Gaza City.*

Was it because there were no more graves in Gaza
that you brought us to the beach to die?

Was it because rubbling us in our houses,
like our cousins, like our futures, like our gods,
would be a bore?

Was it because our cemeteries need cemeteries and
our tombstones need homes?

Was it because our fathers needed more grief?

We were limbs in the wind,
our joy breaking against the shore.
Soccer ball in between our feet
we were soccer in between their feet.
No place to run. No Moses in siege.
Waves stitched together, embroidered, weaved
un-walkable, indivisible, passage—implausible,
on most days we weep in advance.

We looked up to the clouds, got up on clouds.
Here, we know two suns: earth's friend and white phosphorus.
Here, we know two things: death and the few breaths before it.

What do you say to children for whom the Red Sea doesn't part?

Things I Cannot Say

US soldier admits killing unarmed Afghans for sport:
Jeremy Morlock, 23, tells US military court
he was part of a "kill team" that faked combat
situations to murder Afghan civilians.
—*Guardian*, March 23, 2011

Tell our children
the word *soldier*
means what it shouldn't
that terrorists look nothing like
what God on TV says they should.
Tell them
monsters do exist
desiring their skulls—souvenired,
        their limbs—mosaicked,
      and their truths—tarnished again.

Tell them
their names,
        faces,
          and overgrown memories
are landmines—
   landmines
     danced around in terrorism,
            white, uniformed terrorism,
and that pavements are tiled
like a board game
or some sort of mundane, alleged raillery,
and "national heroes" roll dice,
           roll corpses
after posing with them,
homecoming and championed.

Tell them credulous, clueless audiences
will strip them of rights
without thought or prayer.

Boy Sells Gum at Qalandiyah

The question is not morality, the question is money.
That's what we're upset about.

—Toni Morrison

There are bulldozers in these clouds. Bulldozers in their clouds and they bring rain often. A boy at Qalandiyah and they have stolen the wicks of the stars. He shouldn't be outside. Stones will fling themselves in protest.

This Hebrewed land still speaks Arabic. Their drones will rig this. The boy at Qalandiyah selling gum. He shouldn't be outside. He'll be a thrower, a catcher. A bulldozed bulldozer. Often.

What's a boy doing winning bread under gallows? And where's the merit in that? Whose side is God on? Some days it feels like they've unlocked prayer. They prey often.

A man on the sidewalk explains natural selection. As in the boy's grip shouldn't be softened. The man says the boy's walk looks too much like a song and too little like a man walking.

A woman tells him a pen is a sword. What's a pen to a rifle? Another fed him a sonnet. If Shakespeare was from here he wouldn't be writing.

I write about Palestinian boys as if they're older than labor.

The boy is eight, which is twenty-two for Americans. The boy knows this. His mother calls him a man in his nightmares. *You're a man now.* A painter stands in this, collecting strokes. A photographer offers a helping hand. They want to build a museum in his torture. The boy wins the bread knowing he shouldn't be.

He tells the photographer to pay him for his bread; the photographer's bread. For wallets fattened by indigence.

His mother calls him the man of the house. She thinks it makes him feel better about the hunched back he's earned before the 6 a.m. of his life. The gray he's earned before the 6 a.m. of his life. Qalandiyah is gray often.

I drive by. I roll down my window. I buy what I can. *You shouldn't be outside through the fire.* What is fear to the ferocious? I ask him to stop selling gum. He tells me I don't know a thing about this. Don't know a thing about the sun's fingernails clawing the back of his neck.
I'll be quiet then.
I don't know a thing,   truly,
Not a man   yet.   Not a man   often.

Math

My homeland tunnels itself
in an escape to chosen exile.

Blood doesn't wash away
despite the faucets
despite the color of washing.

War Machines Dress Up as Drag Queens

after Audre Lorde

There are many roots.

War machines are coin-operated arcade games,
and your penny sprays and juvenile plays
are just as greedy as a bulldozer's mouth
chewing life into debris for me to dish-wash and make poetry of.

War machines wear lipstick, carry bedazzled purses, and wave
    hellohowareyou?
vogue on said debris / pink faucets. If you ignore the rubble,
this is a haven—its earth is flesh, brown and uncounted.

War machines are American-made, and they are never thirsty /
    rivers in their throats.
American water is brown and dirtied and children famished,
cracked, caged in cages, / in uneducated education.
Surf their boats in drought. Their knuckles stiff, cold is this verse.

I sit here wondering:

Which me will survive bulldozers undoing God?
Which me will soak their hands in these wells?
Which me will console the dead's loved ones with prevention, not
    mourning,
bottle our Jordan River to smack American thirst,
for greed and grief.
Water   stolen or neglected.

Which me will survive all these liberations?

Elderly Woman Falls Asleep on My Shoulder

Elderly Woman on the bus falls asleep on my shoulder.
>   No adjectives in the wind.
Her whistles asleep are choppy, her lungs—I assume—were
>   embroidered with
screams, grainy and grayed.
>   Her phone wakes her up,
her waking up awakens me,
makes me aware of my pocketed-indulgence.
Alert, she asks *Where are we?*
Right before the checkpoint, I say. She responds:
Thank you.

الله يحميك من شر اليهود

"ومن شر المسلمين

Through her scarf I see the Wall;
it exiles her livelihood: selling figs behind a two-hour-something
>   bus ride,
travel permits,
searching and questioning,
tessellated behind bars,
into other bent bodies,
waiting.

Elderly Woman on the bus gets up,
her plastic bags filled with seventy mountains and a river.
I offer a hand. She is concerned about my spine.
Women like her have spined me. I insist, *Let me help you, please.*
She wants to carry thirty-five mountains. I tell her I've got both
bags, not as heavy as they seem

                                  not as heavy as she's lived.
We exit the bus, walking toward the military barrier.
Under occupation, walking feels barefoot.
Here, walking feels like attempting to run
                         in water.

The soldier, blonde and sunburnt, asks her for her permit.
My permit: these wrinkles
older than your country's existence.
My smile is a sun.

The soldier, accented and unhebrew, asks her what's in the bag.
Figs, bitch. What else you want to know?
I stuffed them with storms
and bombs and blows.

      My smile, a gloat.
      I know she had a gun someday, hidden in a wheat bag,
      and I know she hid freedom fighters in her closet—
               warrior woman, za'atar diva.[8]
                 She   may have
                      hid   in her closet, too.

---

8 After Suheir Hammad.

40   Elderly Woman and I pass the checkpoint.
                              Violent vowels in the wind.
     Her back, hunched—her spine, spined me.
     She takes the bags from my hands. *Thank you.*
                              My daughter's waiting to pick me up.
                              May God protect you and the youth
                              around you.
     And before my breath could take a seat,
     she walked away as if she once knew purple shrouds.

Three Women[9]

Atlanta—woman,
black-haired and brown-skinned,
goes to the ER under the bridge
where her hips were cracked open
by men who are sometimes her uncles,
      sometimes her lovers,
      sometimes her choice.
A riot unfolds inside her throat:
poetry made of cuss words and drums.
There is a new planet in her stomach
that feels like swallowing watermelons whole.
The men, wide-knuckled and reaching,
      tell her to push.
Weeping and cradling a sidewalk,
      she pushes out a statistic.

---

9 After Nina Simone's *Four Women* and Suheir Hammad's "4:02 p.m."

Jerusalem—woman,
olive-skinned and olive-selling,
bites down on a metal bar of a military checkpoint.
An ocean spills, unhinged.
Women not midwives or nurses
                    circle around her,
become gods, creating hot water and scissors.
Her mouth is thunderous in its chants:
May God rid us of your fist and rid you of your bullets.
The soldier tells her a chance at an ambulance
is nonexistent, passage requires permit.
The women, fury-filled and shaking,
                    tell her to push.
                    She pushes out a security threat;
                    its first sight is a bullet hole.

Gaza—woman,

lives where bulldozers rest on clouds.
Her hospital bed is her home's rubble,
nothing left of her husband but a bloodied beard.
Nothing around her but refrigerators in trees,
                            furniture defiled,
                    shards of a life, disfigured.
She holds onto the concrete reef
like it's a blanket, like it's Mary's sage.
There is no life without pushing, no life in siege.
Her tongue is a minaret chanting God's name
                            in angry prayer.
The rockets, like rain, tell her to push.
Her thighs spread, pushing out a purple sky,
                            rubbled and silent.
            She weeps,
            cries her inability to mourn another.
            She imagines the umbilical cord,
            a noose.

THREE

Laugh

In the middle of nowhere, I just feel so alone.
—Nicki Minaj

Atlanta taught me poems aren't wood or brick. Poems won't build a house. Atlanta taught me that people will still applaud the bullets puncturing them if they have the right rhythm. This taught me how to look. There are many ways of looking. Doubt is one of them. I learned that success is mathematical and in the past tense. Systems here are snake-like. Shiny scales. I learned how to turn a tub into a mattress. Atlanta taught me how to catch a train, how to miss a train, how to be a train. Atlanta taught me to postpone panic, command rooms. Taught me how to stuff my skull with peacocks. How to walk tall into an argument. Taught me that a dollar is three and a half shekels. That dollars smell amazing. Female rap is the highest form of poetry. White girls are the absolute best at shoplifting, for reasons Atlanta knows. I know shoplifting is gray. Atlanta showed me my first pig carriage in flames. I am learning how to pour gasoline on discourse. This city weds its martyrs, celebrates when they come home. Atlanta taught me that hallway-hellos are not the same as friendship. Jerusalem taught me resilience. Atlanta taught me a different kind. I can now bring the funeral to the podium and laugh. My grandmother taught me *if we don't laugh, we cry.* Atlanta knew that.

Kroger

Someday I know I'll be open armed baby.
　　　　　　　　—B.B. King

I don't have time for an epiphany at Kroger.

　　Don't have time for an epiphany,
& so the epiphany has me.
　　　　　In Atlanta, I stay at Amna's
　　　　on Lynch Ave,

　　　　　　　　　　　　　　　　　bitterness

　　　　　　　in the air.
　　　　　Syn
　　　sleeps next to me.
　　I invert the syntax.
This is the third night,
& I want to kiss her back.
　　　But they're bullying the network
　　　　　for having me, & so I'm writing emails
　　　instead of poems, eating my fist
　　　　　　　in the bathroom,
　　　　I don't want to hear
　　　　about freedom of speech
　　　　or my hostility. I've been
meaning to sleep for a few weeks.

I don't have time for paranoia. Won't flip
rocks or look for merit in the death threats.
If they come for me, let them: I've made
my amends.   Would be content   in
my   coffin. It is those   stuffing
sand in   my mouth   that worry me
most   saying there
are   softer   ways   to   say   this.
Thing is I don't want to be soft. Don't want to
humanize shit. Look at my limbs, look at this
earth.

I've been meaning to eat today
but I spent a thousand mornings since sunrise
insisting upon my integrity.

I don't have time for contextualization. The journalist
interrupts this tragedy to negotiate another. A history whose
debris
is still here: What is a fact in Arabic
              is debatable in English,
              contentious. Thing is, I couldn't care less.
              Say *evict*
              & I'll still say *theft*.
              hyperlink them to death. A reporter
asks if I believe in violence. Irony is a constant guest.
              What's that got to do with anything?
              Another asks what's a holiday like in a tent?
              Who gives a fuck about Christmas and decorations?
              Do I believe in violence?
              Well I don't believe in violation.

I've been meaning to dream.
Closed my eyes in the Uber &
dreamt of the Haitian Revolution.
In Brooklyn, there were three ra-
vens at my door. I am not scared
of snitches. I told myself it was
psychosis. I'm writing this email
so I can abandon the chair. If it
weren't for the smoking, the day
would be a day. I can't wait to be
back. Hope no one will be in a
tent. One day we will write about
dispossession in the past tense.
I've been meaning to take all the
breaths I need. I've been meaning
to write something about hyenas.

Autobiography

Now that I've got a rifle,
take me with you to Palestine
—Nizar Qabbani, sung by Om Kalthoum

I was once bold   tire slashing / security camera snatching
Sister and I   video gamed soldiers over rooftops / Sudoku
Laughter was the motive   less revolution and more liberty
more child's play   played catch with those dogs
until our waists knotted /   cackled ourselves bruised
We hid under blankets until they went away   We were eleven then
I was not a victim   until the world told me so

My teenage years forced me to walk   six inches shorter
Shrunk myself to shrink the comments   Existed without space
There is not   much else I'd like to share about my adolescence
I'm bored with the metaphors   Children threw stones
Sirens were lullabies / fireworks; bombs   and we were sick of it

I was on a podium probably   fourteen or fifteen
talking about the world   like it's in a wheelchair
I'd muffled my ability to slash tires / unscrew fences   and play
for my ability to sulk /   I used to pimp my pain
pawning soldiers for my pleasure /   It was playtime for the twins
Used to pimp my pain   / Now I merely exploit it
I've identified the problem   ashes where should be dust
How do I breathe without smoking?   Inhale without calculating
I need to run like I used to   Mother called them
continent-crossing legs   Zoloft makes my face swell up
a choice between   sanity   and slimness
What does that say about me?   This isn't an epiphany, though
Poems aren't for that

The Day Is Like Butter

You can purchase children
here.

There are reasons why fathers
reason with greed
and mothers affirm this aftermath.
Matters not what children sell for
but that they are sold.
Matters not what is beneath
their chests,
be it sorrow or surrender,
or suns that look like white phosphorous.

A boy was void this morning.
His mother slipped him in the cracks
of a vending machine.
Men with sweet teeth shove
dollar bills in his mouth.

She moistens yeast
to feed open beaks.

This hunger strikes hunt
ruckus rioting here.
God gets up from his barstool
to tend to drunken faithfuls.
He now is on TV
behind tuxedos and talk.
He announces a moving on,
releasing butterflies
from his palms,
singing their swan song.

52   I watch this from my couch,
crocheting myself
a noose.

This is one of those poems that start with "she,"
those poems that break bread with their topics,
offer ibuprofen tablets and tables for those sick with September
    wind
and those sick with G4S.[10]

She told me I looked like I was from Jerusalem
because my face is like those on the news.
I took no offense in what's offensive. *Talent,*
I told her. *That's talent that you knew. I'm from the land of Christ*

cross-wearing woman. I'm from a land torn and abused
by the company you work for. I spat out storms coaxing her into war,
but what war could she wage when the only wage we know
is minimal? What war could she wage when choice

left the equation—when voice was robbed
from our throats? From her throat, a cough evades conversation.
I get her a pill or two, offer water,
ask about her maze-like commute of buses and trains,
teeth aching and lungs weaker by the tick.

---

10 G4S is a security contractor with a strong presence in the Israeli govern-
ment. It helps run prisons, police training centers, checkpoints, settlements
and military bases. Though it is contracted to provide equipment and services
to Israeli prisons, G4S is deeply complicit in Israeli use of mass incarceration.
Many of the 500–700 Palestinian children who are arrested, detained and
prosecuted by "Israel" are held in G4S-equipped prisons.

54   She tells me her commute is serpentine:
curvaceous, elongated, carnivorous. *That's talent,*
I tell her. I praise her metaphor. She tells me she knows poetry
like a distant cousin.

"How far is Palestine?" She asks. It's a fifteen-hour plane ride away,
a dozen unresolved UN resolutions away, a few history lessons
    away, a hundred and
some military checkpoints away, too much G4S-provided asphyx-
    iation.
Crossing back and forth like that,

that's talent, she says.

Park Benches with Teeth

I live by people whose beds
                are a pillow and a blanket,
                      a bus seat,
            a seatless bus stop,
          a cold hard pavement,
      a potential they slept on or
were robbed of. I live by people
whose dreams are
                adequate,
      but not selfish enough,
whose dreams are without adjectives,
                    postponed,
            pocket-sized, and
famished.
Told to find the glass in the sand,
hunger dreams of spat out
generosity
and cement
defanged

Not a dollar is a blanket
not a guilt is a table
to place meals on or
discuss
their humanity
around.

Not a sound nor a nod
can make my fury monetary
when I hear shivers crackling like fires
from my bedroom.

Not a poem nor a post is enough to turn
                    the post they live under into a tent.
Not one of them has bent, gathered our prayers, and weaved them
into a home or a hoodie.

I live by people for whom ceilings are luxuries,
        for whom park benches have teeth at night,
                pointing upwards and into sleep's flesh,
        and for whom jail cells are mandatory motels
                    for when the city decides to dust its pillows.
Every morning I pass them by,
tessellated under bridges and into performative priorities
                    with hooded identities,
                mostly of certain wrists:
                            wrists that bend or
                                    slice open or
            contemplate death   scarred by cuffs or
            leashed to a misfortune or a debt.

I live by people whose solace
                    is a fruit well-known
                    and spoken ill of,
            whose solace is sins, sex,
            histories of moving bricks
                    or throwing bricks
                    at uniformed pigs,
whose solace is a reminiscing of a bed.

I live by people whose mattresses   are memory,
                                    are substance,
                                    are made featherless,
                                            fatherless

with springs, elusive
                and marching upwards and into the
backs of their necks, their spines

                              troubled, unfixed,
their stories come unhinged, their eyes
after   a dollar or a supper
  but not a dollar nor a supper,
          not a protest nor a pretense.
Not a protest nor a pretense.

No Poetry in This

There is no poetry in suicide and
    no poetry in cigarettes,
yet
so many poets break their lines with threats of triggers,
        break their lines   with cliffs.
    Poets break their necks below cliffs.
    Many find refuge in rifts.
    Many find rhymes in death and sing
                a little of a lullaby—a dwelling,
a swimming in mourning,
whisper in each other's ears, around writing tables, their wills.
There is no beauty in this.

And They Leave and Never Leave[11]

I have studied the tight curls on the back of your neck
moving away from me,
and I have waited in stance,
   wilted for distance,
    rooted in the cracks
of my ceramic bathroom tiles,
    staring into the mirror,
    waiting for your face
       to exit me.
I have memorized the patterns of breaths in which
your voice invaded my throat,
      gloated that you
       are leaving me.
Atlanta put me in a taxi.
     Transit became home.
This time, in Palestine,
there were no pomegranates in trees
   but suitcases
    situated by storm,
and I have fled
a different kind of heartache
   than that my mother
    had pickled and jarred
     and served for me.

---

11 After Audre Lorde's "Movement Song."

Amal Hayati

يا حب غالي   wake in the crux of a confluence امل حياتي
there are two dead horses
under this mattress
rubbled which you
sleep

ما ينتهيش   يا حب غالي

chain the carcasses
to your waist bleed
pulling them to the pick-up truck
red gravel
gnaws the hide

the highway picks up
three women in leopard print
party city blonde
they are
passengers for a pause

hope of my life
a precious love
* that doesn't end*

the pattern   an autobiography
your aunt   pomegranate
                              red hair

grooming   muffles
the maiming   of your side
rust   rivets
                          the pancreas

anatomy of shackles
interrupted   in a   barbershop

take all of my years
but today
let me live

62

خليني
جميك خلين
في حضن قلبك
خليني

on the road
    the horses
    rustle
        the trunk
    a nagging
        cavity

eyebrows   are falcons
    are wings
            blinking
is flirting
        with concrete

    if only   the bumps
        could awaken
                the race
            in them
            your dear horses
dead
        since March
    of some year

keep me
by your side, keep me
in your heart's embrace
keep me

and let me dream
let me
I hope my time
doesn't wake me

finger   coils
the radio   it drowns
in a bath   Om Kalthoum muffled
in water

يا حبيب مبارح
وحبيب دلوقتي
يا حبيبي لبكرا
ولآخر وقتي

memory   melted
the clock   you mold
your past   picking
at   scabs

sand   thickens   from blood
   a straight line   into
                          submergence
the horses
            linger
onshore
            then   there is
      the pull

the lover of yesterday
and lover of right now.
my beloved for tomorrow
and the rest of my days

the initial choice: tie the chains
without emphasis   on liberty

once in the blue   deadweights act
                     as deadweights do

إحكيلي، قلي
ايه من الأماني ناقصني تاني
وانا بين إيديك؟

narrate to me
tell me
what wishes am I lacking
if I'm in your arms?

wake

rubbled
on a mattress
in vast grass

python
embraces
you
then tightens

wind
withdrawn
your jaw
at peace
at last

خليني
جمبك خليني
في حضن قلبك
خليني

Keep me / by your side, keep me. / In your heart's embrace / keep me

FOUR

Anti-Biography

I don't believe in capitalism or socialism,
or any ism that gives my mother a fuss.
                                    —Jackie Braje

I am but my credentials, apparently,
                    in third person
                    in pretense.

I am but Jerusalem, too.
Published by way of

                              their remorse
                                    snipers to my spine
                                    bombs women children etc.
My apologies for the inverted syntax
I am reluctant to say what I write about:
                    I don't know anymore.
                    The question is about the earth—
                              primates over prose

Most days   I'm in psychosis   spine to my storms
                                            bait to my rage
                                            tired metaphors.
I think identity is corny.
That would have enraged me at seventeen.
My current beliefs would have—
                    except for the rifles
we all agree on the rifles.

I am but the institution, the prestige, the watermelon.
Most of that poetry is theater over thunder.
Most days I'm pulling pythons off my ribs.

I don't hope for much more than what my grandmother hoped for.
Most of the rest is مسخرة   How do you translate مسخرة؟

I am but all that performance.
Who took poets off park benches to put commercials for poets on
    park benches?
Who took poets off my shelves to put pills where poets once were?
            I won't sit on a recliner
            and pay $200 an hour
            to make villains out of coffee stains.

I gulp metaphors without counting.
My poems become mosaics   unintentionally,
messy rooms   habitually.

                    A cluttered bedroom isn't poetic
                    it's melodrama.

I am but my love for my land, by the way,
        I have chosen you, my homeland, in love and in obedience
                            in secret and in public.

In truth I'm ashamed of my dreams.
There are those who dream of seeing the ocean,
Palestinian men who saw grave before gravel,
            the coffin before the coast.

Newspaper blank commissions:
"The Psychological Effects of Occupation."
I have never once felt free anywhere:
not with the Jordanian passport;

> not in Santa Monica, the American Tel Aviv;
> not in New York, the American Tel Aviv;
> not in Tel Aviv, the American Tel Aviv.

*

I am but my nostalgia,
        my sick homesickness.
Bike through Brooklyn:
Jerusalem neighborhoods
Radio "Israel."
        This is a yearning for rage.   I'm in Stockholm.

What else goes into a bio?
                On Judgement Day, God asks your parents
about you.
I am but my obedience to my mother.
رضاكي يا أمي
God said it,   apparently.

I keep my secrets to keep her sane.

Not breaking cycles if that'll break her heart.

She's had a tough life.

These are her years to rest.

Why are you explaining the morning to a rooster?

They wouldn't know the truth if it knew them. This is a yawning pattern. The oils, the soils, the lands, the hands. A penetrative bureaucracy. Poverty, a circus. If I squeezed their bread in my hand, my blood would drip out of it. You and I became the other, the minority. The word *injustice* lost half its heft. It seemed sudden. A pimple before the party. You pleaded for history at the party. Let me tell you, they are some stubborn acne.

The comedy, though, is in the language. The things they deafen and defeat. They renamed the streets, the tombs. Hell, whole cemeteries. You want to tell them how our feet take on to the streets? You want to tell them what land means to us? They couldn't run in my rhetoric. Run as in rule, as in campaign, as in sprint. I have gathered my bricks, a synonym for teaching. Why do you speak of the massacre at the party? You want to give out mirrors like they're brochures?

They want us to show gratitude. Otherwise we'd ruin their gravity. They spit as they say my name. They acknowledge they're on occupied land. Irony just sits there. A negated graffiti. If pain were a man, I'd give him a hand or two. They've had a long run. Couldn't run like that in my imagination. Why do you tell them a story they wrote? In third grade, school taught me about the emperor's clothes. Don't your hands tire of gesturing?

They cannot see you. This morning the phoenix made sure its ashes were damp enough to never rise again. At a certain point, the metaphor tires. At a certain point, I'll grab a brick. At a certain point, I wrote it in the email. They brought divinity to the crime scene to avoid justice. Justice should eat something.

We're mere words on their resumes. The TSA people are way nicer. These people make me feel in third person. Over there, minarets call for prayer, and here, their mouths recite emails. One of them promised to put my rags in the museum. One of them let me know his analysis of my constant hostility. Coughs to conversation. Blame it on the war zone. He couldn't believe I'm from there, called me a flower in cement, earth erupting from a rock. What a miracle. What a thing pretending has become. I stood on the roof and assassinated all the adjectives.

Will the caterpillar escape the genre?

They talk about me and say, *those folks*. I'm exultant though. I sit at the party and the feedback hesitates. Oh, I forgot to tell you, I spoke of the massacre at the party.

Did the war wage itself?

—Sinan Antoon

We should continue to call our dead martyrs.

Foes rifled that word so we emphasize our neutrality. [Martyr] wasn't participating in the fighting, human rights in em dashes. [Martyr] without monkeys or motives.

[Martyrs] who swept airplanes off balconies, [martyrs] fanatic, Biden livid at the Palestinians once more. [Martyrs] are a talking point.

[Martyr] I knew in high school waited for his fangs to grow.

[Martyr] was in love scraping underneath the bus.

[Martyr] at the bar and he was gone in two shots. [Martyr] my cousin couldn't even choose the fight. [Martyr] at the border, snort off of the rifle. Rifle to the [martyr], coin to the vending machine.

[Martyr] never knocked.

[Martyr's] breaks unwed the concrete, and the forensics agree, but [martyr] is in the fridge still. His mother is parsley going bad.

[Martyr] my black rooster announcing the morning before the pigs.

[Martyr] brought to the sink and washed. [Martyr's] death ten years later the government sends out Hallmark cards, and Washington spat on Mandela a few breaths before it kissed him.

[Martyr] bought three oranges and never made the juice.

Crows

If you're not careful, the newspapers will have you hating the
people who are being oppressed and loving the people who are
doing the oppressing.

—Malcolm X

There will come a day
I'll walk in the crevices
of crows conversing
off of clichéd avenues.
I will get into the elevator
blurry and bowed-head,
thankful not to be dead
in this building of genocidal rhetoric,
rheology—my strategy—as I ask about the office
where opinion shapers
rhyme my country with its cancer,
And I will flip the conference table
        on the conference itself.
I will tell them
I have mailed you fire last week, did you receive my flames?
They will imagine a rifle on my tongue
and fix themselves fetuses in the corner,
cover their ears in fear of the firecrackers
and horses and rockets I've stuffed in my bag.
                They will heave their proclamation,
                  heed my "perspective" of current affairs,
I'll hold my word to one of the men's heads.
and he'll tremble as I press against his temple and say,
Say it.
Say it.
Say my name without spitting.

Lice

Suheir Hammad told me   *grief the teacher.*
                    I said   *grief the thief.*
It taught me wishing myself a monkey
picking lice off my brother's head
instead of   this here   tuxedos and talk.

I indulge in apology
        sorry at large.

I'm often to blame
keeping a dozen dead horses under my bed.
remorseful poems to those illiterate in remorse.
This isn't even   a metaphor
        not even a jab   not a stone.

My friends tell me I need to be talking,
explaining the slayer to the slain—Doctor,
what if I told you I distrust
civilization and the civilized,
that I'd rather   pick lice off my brother's head
        than   pick the sanity off my own?

Grief the teacher and shame the compass.
        I am often moved not moving.
I'd rather snatch the apple
out my own throat   I want to
            snatch the apple
out my own throat. I want my voice
voiceless. Place gems in my sockets
and I'll pretend I can see.

English calls sentimentality tacky,
                seldom allows sirens a breath,
and I insist on this oxygen.

I can only describe this guilt
with similes that would invalidate it.
I no longer want to language, no longer
                want to tongue.

The past few years I've treated airports
like funeral homes—
dragging my dead horses onboard
new cities   new drones.
I wish I were a landlord
to the tenants in my head. Wish I could
pimp my pain   and harden.
Grief the teacher   and I never learn.

Where Am I From Jerusalem?

after Naomi Shihab Nye

If you tilt your head just slightly
It's ridiculous:
Tigers astray,
hyenas in military wear.
A girl walked off.
The men scoffed.
I wasn't there; I was told
they ate the last words
still.

In Jerusalem,
a boy's sun is stolen.
No longer a spine.
A fly in the ear,
he's twenty-two years and spinning.
If this were New York
he would have laughed as they did it.

God at the drugstore.
Adderall, of course
The horse fell off.[12]
This tent-taught tact.
A lingering wind.

---

12 After Mahmoud Darwish.

Never has there been a battle that ended:
You wake up a word
in somebody's throat.
Eight months later,
a stuck elevator.
The math chews on.

I can shoplift a mattress
every time I need one.
Dry bread unveils the world.
Gender becomes uneventful

9 p.m. a televised circus,
two clowns opinionating,
laughter in a wallet.
I count rent before teeth.
Pocket-sized dreams
bite to the burn
& so culture becomes as boring
as a scarecrow to birds that know.

When God made me,
he bought the store.
The problem is I want what I want.
And what I want
is sick airplanes away

Where am I from Jordan?
From a bus of sweat
towards Jericho & towering upwards
straightening?

Where am I from falcons on my eyebrows?
From cigarettes and earthquakes?
A face reveals itself
in Damascus Gate.
I used to duck for snipers
as my mother pointed them out in the trees.

Where am I from serenity
And butchering my alarms?
Where am I from jasmines
and the fig tree?
From plants prostituted by poetry?

Where am I from awakening?
From friends that humble this pretension?
From more shoulders to this heft?
From unsolicited help?

There are prophets
in psych wards,
plowing the ground.
A crucifixion in asterisks.
To wait by a phone
is to be killed.

Where am I from grunts?

A stoning with a soda can?
I sit on the bus and wait for my fangs to grow.

Where am I from a necessary hostility?
From fangs grown?
From fingers orchestrating the room?
Where am I from Bethlehem?

Mary gave me a mattress,
sage.
And for three months
I slept on a broken covenant.

At first, it was in a suitcase,
maybe in a taxi.
Last I saw my heart
teenagers with rifles
in green uniforms
made me throw it up at Gilo.

Mary took me in.
I need to thank her once more.
Comical is
crows offended by stones.

Where am I from offense?

Somewhere in this poem
Edward Said throws a rock.

What's a resumé
to a tank?

What candy are we thrown?
What will my kids learn
from a world
ignorant of them?

Where am I from Jerusalem
and dreams that brown teeth?
In the 70s
hash was here.
You're handed or handcuffed.
Nowadays the policemen
come to the garden at night.

Where am I from the garden
and all that life in the grass?

Where am I from Jerusalem,
from that "State"?
From hyenas ambushing ambulances
and from blood on the streets?

Adrenaline to apathy.
Some days I hear them
carving their cities under my skin,
and hope I don't collapse.

Where am I from forgetting?
From rage in a speakerphone?
From horses stomping on a protest,
From hoses raining on their riot?

Nadia collected the plastic chairs
as eighty special-force clowns
shook the street.
Storm.

My ribcage between a pole and a police baton.
She blamed herself
for the blue in my bones,
God rest her soul.

Where am I from her soul?

Where am I from the grave?

I sat there in my adolescence,
watching the sky turn bruised.
Next time I'm in Palestine
my grandmother's name will be on stone.

It's finding the joke in the jasmine.

Bush

Shoe to the head
I've never felt pride
like this.
Bush   shoe to the head.
Mother was in the kitchen
Saddam in a noose,
handsome.   Apologies
wrapped in tweed.

I wish a snake would swallow me.
I wish the earth would split & swallow me.

Bush   towers astray
I don't believe in
conversation or reconciliation
or crows gouging out my eyes.
My father was a million fire ants.
Millionaires giving out charity
as if it's charity when
cents don't make a dent.
We're supposed to say thanks.
They acknowledge
our blood on their hands.

I wish a snake would swallow me.
I wish the earth would split & swallow me.

Bush   sits beside me on the train.
Iraq veteran cites his fear of fireworks.
They think they're the only ones
with PTSD.   We're literate
in peeling off our own skin to sleep.
          We live like walking debris,
swallow snakes, swallow whole pharmacies,
wrap our spines around the fingers
of bank tellers, while Bush is at a Joanne's
picking the perfect blue.

The Biggest Punch Line of All Time

Great Britain was beaten. You will be beaten too!
—Rifqa El-Kurd

Rifqa took from me my molotovs.
If not a metaphor
they'd make a good vase for jasmines,
a good jazz for the dinner table,
where revolution is TV volume lowered
to make room for conversation.

Over the years   her fingers thinned,
veins like vines.
Verandas required less wandering
and Teta gave up the remote.

Sheikh on the screen babbles about relief.
It is what comes after patience. *After patience
there is but a grave*, Teta says.

Why cradle a century-old woman
whose punch lines are still intact?

My mother
is her cane.
When not a metaphor, her cane is
the edge of a bed or the edge of a sentence.
She clings onto physics and wit.
Her cane is
never a stick for the elderly. She who once knew
purple shrouds, who once knew
clouds as lint in her hair,
shall not bow her head. It's a fight really

4 a.m., and my parents are screaming hospitals.
Teta fell again.

She's OK. Alhamdulillah. A hundred years
tightroping the distance between pride and self-respect.
I grew up in a circus. I grew up in ERs
and death after the ER
was uncommon so I never held breath or hands.
                              Hope for me
was a serendipitous outcome, always.
Teta walks fragile.
She's a straight spine in theory.
I got from her   her hunch
and her hunch.

Last July, she asked how we're getting home.
On our bikes, I said, giggling.
You take your bike, and I'll take my horse.
Her punch lines intact   her smirk unwavering.

I assign imagination to memory:
molotovs in Fendi bags,
                              pamphlets in python shoes,
silk scarves masquerading rampage,
a grandson fascinated by both rebellions.

Teta remembers what she has to:
rifles in rice bags,
bellies split open,
women mistaking pillows for offspring,
men sirening the street performing ardor,
women whose gods no longer respond,
men emasculated by refugee status.
She does not remember my name;
unkindness is much more memorable   than blood
She remembers seven decades later
what martyred her homeland the first time.

Political conviction sticks.
Chants chandeliering her subconscious

Habibi? Why are you in America?
School.
God bless you. Mohammed who?
Why America? Be careful! Tell them,
"America is the reason." Tell them, "Drink the sea."
Let them ride their tallest horses.
Jerusalem is ours.

The biggest punch line of all time.

Sheikh Jarrah Is Burning

If "Israel" is venom in a snake's fang
our youth have defanged the snake.

—**Abu Arab**

If the first sentence is the skunk water, it's overwritten for the tear gas in Abu Ali's living room. The Nakba asserts Sheikh Jarrah is not an exception to the rule. A microcosm of settler colonialism, I've been telling the media, ethnic cleansing, apartheid, a hell, whatever you want to call it!

This is the second month of the blockade. The media won't call it illegal. Zionist philanthropy carves out its home in my spine. American settlers find their way into the front yard, and their billionaires take us to court. Their laws are daggers. Their laws are hungry. Armed colonizers peacock around my street with impunity.

After the protest, they put up cement barriers. No journalists, no medics. The pig calls me by my name before he asks for my ID. No entry. The settlers walk in, no questions. Barricades for them are hypothetical. I told an American reporter this is apartheid, but she's not entirely convinced. I look at the cuts she sustained, jumping over my neighbor's fence.

Early May: Mahmoud's head was under a fascist's knee. If only he didn't have the rifle and the baton! Jana was standing in her house, on May 19, when a Zionist shot her in the back. She is sixteen soon. Her spine will recover, I hope. It is those who are spineless who cannot buy themselves a spine. They broke Saleh's leg. Stun grenades turn midnight into dawn. Military horses storm through us. The skunk water truck shoots at our fruit trees. Skunk sticks, its evidence blistered on Muna's hands. They keep chanting for our death. Some of us sleep in our shoes, others sleep through the waged war.

A cavalry came to confiscate our balloons. They looked ridiculous getting off their high horses to climb up the settlers' ladder, untangling the balloons from the electricity wires. We laugh as much as we can before the teargas. There's a circus in their brutality. At the interrogation they asked me how we dare paint Palestinian flags on a children's faces. They asked what's my problem with the police? *Nothing*, I answered. Nothing but the cuffs on my hands and feet. The bruises and the rifle butts. They're arresting everyone and their mother. Arresting broomsticks and donkeys. Arresting schoolgirls with Palestinian flags. Our beloved speaker system. A kite, a hat, my threshold for shock.

A dozen Kyle Rittenhouses patrol my street. Cowards if not for their M-16s. They attacked us with rocks and dispossession. We retaliated with plastic chairs in lieu of the rockets. I stood in awe of the hail. The settlers stole our chairs, and the cops sat on them. I called this collusion. My journalist friend didn't believe me until a settler gestured to a cop to kick her out of the neighborhood. I gave her a cigarette in lieu of an "I told you so."

The youth remind me with firework spectacle: decolonization is not an abstract theory. See: The soldier with a stone in his fascist face. The colonizer car in flames. Surveillance cameras smashed. "Checkpoints" emptied out of their gatekeepers. I stand in awe of the hail.

My grandmother, Rifqa El-Kurd passed away on Tuesday, June 16, 2020. She was 103 years old.

Each day after school, my grandmother would welcome me at the door with jasmines wrapped in Kleenex. I grew up in her wisdom, and my poetry reflects that. She is the axis to my actions, the orchestrator of my cadence. She cameos in my poetry and praxis.

My grandmother lived through wars and then some. She was older than Zionist colonization. For this, she was hailed as the "icon of Palestinian resilience" by Jerusalemites. During the 1948 Nakba, she left her Haifa home meticulously clean, not knowing she was readying it for its colonizers. A refugee, cast with her children from city to city, she finally settled in Jerusalem, only to be confronted with the Naksa[13] and the theft of Jerusalem, and, in her last days of life, the imminent seizure of the West Bank. She died amid the chaos of the "Deal of the Century" and Zionist plans to make Palestinian subjugation permanent and call it a state. Her activism led her from court halls to protests to hospitals. Relentless, she worked until survival became a funny story to tell with what remains of the family.

In 2009, Zionist settlers, adorned with backpacks as if going on a weekend camping trip, entered our homes in occupied Jerusalem, escorted by Israeli occupation forces. They claimed that our home was theirs. After a tumultuous battle with two colonial committees in Israeli occupation courts, the settlers seized half of our home. Their takeover was part of a broader effort to ethnically cleanse the entirety of the Sheikh Jarrah neighborhood. We were among 180

---

13 The term Naksa (Arabic for setback) refers to the 1967 War (June 5–11, 1967) between "Israel" on one side and Syria, Jordan, and Egypt on the other. In this war, "Israel" occupied the rest of Palestine (the West Bank, including the eastern part of Jerusalem and the Gaza Strip), Egypt's Sinai Peninsula (returned in the 1980s), and the Golan Heights (still under occupation). The Naksa marks the second half of the Zionist colonial project.

Palestinian families facing dispossession orders from Israeli courts that claimed that our homes were built on Jewish lands. Across the street from us, we watched the Ghawi family, thrown out of their home, set up a makeshift camp on the street on their land where Zionist colonizers settled.

As a child, I witnessed my grandmother, eighty-something at the time, as a freedom fighter, herself an ambulance, treating tear-gassed protesters with yogurt and onions. In 2009, I saw her rally her body against heavily armed and American-accented settlers and police in our yard, as they claimed our land as theirs by divine decree. As if God were a real estate agent.

Because the colonizers moved into half of the house, separated from my family only by drywall, our home's 2009 confiscation was highly publicized. The house became an international hub to which solidarity activists and curious liberals alike made pilgrimages. But my grandmother refused to be a humanitarian case for gazing eyes. She was not a clueless woman. She was always ready with her talking points and historical facts. *Are you American?* she would ask some of the visitors, before letting them know that the United States is largely to blame for our homelessness and statelessness. She would say the same to people from England. *We don't want your sympathy, we want your action*, she would say. Her punch lines intact.

My grandmother suffered from dementia for a year before her death. But despite sometimes forgetting my name, her political conviction stuck. The atrocities she witnessed blanketed her sub-conscious, so much so that, amid her memory's decay, her stories of the Nakba were still highly detailed, her comments hurled at TV news coherent and complex.

Her wit stuck too. In her last July, visiting my aunt in Nablus, my grandmother did not know where we were and asked how we're getting back to Jerusalem. *On our bikes*, I answered her jokingly. *You take your bike and I'll come on my horse*, she retorted. Her smirk unwavering.

In truth, I am not ready to eulogize her. Even in writing this, I find myself having trouble with tenses. Some people cannot exist in the past tense. For a hundred years, she walked a tightrope between pride and self-respect. My grandmother taught me everything I know about dignity. She taught me how to launch my sentences like missiles, how to be resilient. Even in the face of displacement, monetary punishment, tens of trials, and threats of imprisonment, she persisted. *I will only agree to leave Sheikh Jarrah to go back to my Haifa house that I was forced to flee in 1948*, she famously said, demanding her right of return.

I do not know when I will digest her death. The day she passed, social media was effusive with condolences. Blogs and news outlets mourned the death of "Palestine's jasmine tree," and much like the trees, my grandmother died standing. This, my first collection of poetry, *Rifqa*, I publish to honor and immortalize her. I know that Palestine will not let its icon of resilience die. Some people just do not die. I can already imagine her wrinkled face etched in the lines of stones in the Old City. I know her roots are entangled underneath my every step.

A few years ago, my grandmother and I watched men preach about patience on TV. *Be patient! For after patience comes relief!* My grandmother responded, *After patience comes the grave!*

She demanded justice all her life, and much like James Baldwin, who could not live six decades more to see the "progress" he was constantly promised, "progress" has taken more than my grandmother's time. We are yet to see the fruits of our decades-old patience.

I am heartbroken that she died without having seen a free Palestine, though I promise her that the grandchildren have not forgotten. This fight is a revolution until victory. Rifqa embodied that until her very last breath.

Afterword
Lest There Be Unclarity

After all, in the final analysis, man is a cause.
—Ghassan Kanafani

Years ago, following a friend's advice, I laid out dozens of printed poems on the floor to look for a common theme. And there she was—my grandmother Rifqa—in almost every poem. She had embodied the Nakba's plurality[14] and stoically witnessed its crushing continuity. She had inserted herself into my interpretations. She became my moral compass. I'd measured everything by the tragedy she so stubbornly refused. Naturally, she was the root of the poem.

My mother, Maysoon, had been a poet, too, regularly publishing in *Al-Quds* newspaper. Her drafts would consistently be sent back after the Israeli military censor[15] had red-penciled them. After a certain point, she and my father would entertain themselves by guessing the sections of her writing that would be cut. I learned that poetry is planting a bomb in a garden—a masquerade. Language is not free.

Jerusalem was a perpetual reminder of the Zionist occupation's actuality and terror, and my grandmother represented a time in which it didn't exist. And she clung onto that time.

---

14 Like many Palestinians, my grandmother faced Zionist violence, dispossession, and ethnic cleansing in dozens of cities across historical Palestine, during varied periods, like 1944, 1948, 1956, 1967, 2000, 2008, etc.

15 Censorship is a tactic that Zionism has historically heavily utilized. In 1972, the Israeli Mossad assassinated Palestinian novelist Ghassan Kanafani. In 1988, the *Los Angeles Times* reported that Israel banned *Al-Quds* newspaper from circulating for forty-five days, after the paper ran a story identical to the one the Israeli newspapers ran. In recent years, hundreds of Palestinians were incarcerated because of social media posts, most famous of whom is poet Dareen Tatur, who was sentenced to five months' imprisonment after she'd shared a poem titled "Resist, My People Resist" on Facebook.

It wasn't only reminiscing. Most of the time, my grandmother would orate Nakba narratives, discrediting the circumstance, damning the outcomes. Sometimes despondent, sometimes elbowing her sorrow. She lived in cold, stale anger that she might have processed decades ago had she the chance to catch her breath. I became the sole anthropological authority, reclaiming her relic, living in cold anger that has sat deep within me and shaped my cynicism. I realize now that a poetry book formed as a didactic tool became one whose merit relies on negating the politics of appeal.

I may have been sixteen or seventeen when I started writing this book, eleven or twelve when I began writing grammatically incorrect, typo-ridden poems. Poetry was an itch to contextualize, to inform, to hinge severed limbs onto the people to whom they once belonged, to allow those people nuance.

At first, I made two mistakes.

The first was that I trained myself to use "unbiased" words. What I'd refer to in Arabic as an "entity" would become a "state." Striving for a vocabulary void of accusation, I replaced "arrogate" with "confiscate," "dispossess" with "evict," and "lie" with "allege." This phenomenon is common among writers writing about Palestine, writers who worship the mythology of objectivity instead of satirizing it. There's this naïve belief that Palestinians will acquire credibility only once they've amassed respectability. I did this to appear rational and unhostile. The truth, however, is very hostile.

The second mistake is what I will call "humanization": I portrayed my people only in the ways that adhere to ethnocentric civility, robbing them of their agency. It is to "women and children" Palestinians to death—to infantilize Palestinians in hopes of determining that, indeed, they deserve liberation.

This practice of infantilization stems from the ahistorical depictions of Palestinians and Zionists in the media. Ironically, the regime with one of the world's most lethal armies does not require humanization. The world can grieve Israeli loss without qualifiers, despite the disparities in the death toll. In contrast, we must qualify our dead with reminders of their nonviolence, humane professions, and disabilites. A Palestinian man cannot just die. For him to be mourned, he must be in a wheelchair or developmentally delayed, a medical professional, or noticeably elderly at the very least. Even then, there are questions about the validity of his victimhood.

Having lived in the United States for four years, I realize that much of what I try to expose is already blatant. This indifference to Palestinian death exists despite morality and "human rights." Humanization, more often than not, does the exact opposite of what it alleges. I no longer feel the responsibility to give humans eyes for humanity.

In my revisions of this book, I tried, as much as I could, to make sure that the women mentioned are active participants in its rhetoric and have a say in the poem, that they aren't just trembling in their victimhood like sticks in the wind, that they aren't mere vehicles for extracting empathy.

The transition from naïveté to blatancy stemmed from tackling things at the root. I knew to address the disease rather than punish the symptom. Punished symptoms worsen. The validity of my resistance is no longer an interesting topic. My mother once said in a (later censored) poem: *Does a rooster seek permission to crow?* My political convictions crystalized when I began peacocking my people's claim to dignity instead of burrowing within it.

I conceptualized and conceived the bulk of this project in Palestine, namely Jerusalem, Bethlehem, and Ramallah; and good portions of it in the United States, mostly Atlanta, Georgia, where I attended college; and Amman, Jordan, where I was in labyrinthine transit between here and there. Those disparate geographies forced me to situate myself in questions larger than politics. The human condition, arrested by a paralyzing sorrow or cold anger, remained the most interesting aspect of writing this book.

Above all, although this book isn't an attempt to free Palestine, its central thesis is that Palestine, in its historical entirety, must be liberated by any means necessary. Accelerated normalization of Zionism and Nakba denial has made it imperative to sit stubbornly in my political convictions. There isn't a more urgent statement to make. There isn't a cause more critical. In my brief twenty-two years of personhood, I have seen Palestine dwindle in size and spirit like a decaying loved one.

I refuse to wait in the wreck.

Acknowledgments

"Autobiography" was first published in *Vacuuming Away Fire*, published by the Savannah College of Art and Design in 2020.

"This Is Why We Dance" was first published as a video on *Al-Jazeera English*.

"Born on Nakba Day"; "Elderly Woman Falls Asleep on My Shoulder" (formerly, "Figs, Bitch!"); "Things I Cannot Say," (formerly, "To Afghan Children,"); "No Moses in Siege,"; "The Day Is like Butter"; and "No Poetry in This" were first released on *Bellydancing on Wounds*, a poetry-oud album with Clarissa Bitar, 2019. Available wherever you stream music.

"The Biggest Punch Line of All Time" and "Farewell, Palestine's Jasmine" (formerly, "My Grandmother: Icon of Palestinian Resilience") were originally published in the *Nation*.

Gratitude

Thank you to the abundance of people who helped this book come to life. I'd originally had a list of friends, loved ones, and teachers to whom I'll forever be indebted, but I chose to take the list out in fear of neglecting to mention one of them. They know who they are, and they know I am immensely grateful for them.

Many thanks to Maya Marshall and Rami Karim for editing this book. And thank you to aja monet for advocating for this book, and to Haymarket for publishing it.

About the Author

Mohammed El-Kurd is an internationally touring and award-winning poet and writer from Jerusalem, occupied Palestine. He has been featured in numerous international outlets like the *Guardian*, the *Nation*, *Washington Post*, MSNBC, *New York Times*, CNN, and elsewhere. Mohammed earned a BFA in writing from the Savannah College of Art and Design and is currently pursuing an MFA in poetry from Brooklyn College. El-Kurd is also a visual artist and printmaker. This is his first book.